Morgan 4/4

MORGAN OWNERS HANDBOOK

Ford and Fiat Engines
1968 - 1985

Chassis Number: B1600 - B5133 - Ford

Chassis Number: F6002 - F6956 - Fiat

ISBN 9781783181858

Morgan Motor Company Limited
Pickersleigh Road, Malvern Link, Worcestershire WR14 2LL England
Tel: 01684 573104 / 573105 www.morgan-motor.co.uk

FOREWORD

The object of this book is to provide the owner with a clear picture of the car and its needs. Technical terms have been avoided wherever possible.

Each car is carefully built and tested, but the continued satisfaction of the owner is largely in his own hands. The best cars will not run well unless careful attention is paid to their upkeep.

To gain the maximum pleasure and performance from your Morgan, lubricate regularly, keep all nuts, bolts and screws tight and thereby reduce rattle and unwanted noises, and lastly keep brakes properly adjusted and in good working order. Alterations and adjustments from the standard specification are not recommended but, should it seem necessary, our Service Department will be pleased to give advice if contacted.

In all communications relating to Service and Spares please quote the chassis and engine number.

The information in this handbook is as close as possible to the correct information about your car. Continuing development means that changes are made all the time and some of these may not be covered by this book. Errors and omissions are avoided, but cannot be ruled out.

CONTENTS

Touring Advice

The high compression ratio of your car has been designed to use 97 Research octane petrol, 4-star rating in the United Kingdom. This fuel is not always obtainable in some European countries. When your car is to be used in these countries where 97 Research octane petrol is unobtainable, it is essential that adjustments be made to retard the ignition timing to avoid damage being caused to the engine. Your Morgan agent is equipped to make the necessary adjustments, or alternatively advice can be obtained from the factory if the following information is given.

    (i) Chassis No. of Car Stamped on top face of chassis cross member under seat.

    (ii) Serial No. of Engine and compression ratio which will be found stamped at the rear left of the engine adjacent to the back of the top rocker cover or the centre of left cylinder head.

    (iii) The country or countries in which it is intended to use the car.

The adjustments recommended should be carried out by your Morgan Distributor, prior to you departure. Failure to observe this requirement will be taken into consideration should any claim be made under the terms of the Warranty in respect of any engine damage resulting from using fuels other than those of 97 research octane rating. Research octane is the currently accepted method of octane rating designation employed throughout the industry.

THE IMPORTANCE OF ALWAYS USING THE CORRECT TYPE OF SPARKING PLUGS CANNOT BE OVERSTRESSED.

Index

SECTION ONE
General Specification - Ford and Fiat Engine

DATA - FORD ENGINE

Chassis Number	On offside top of cross member under front seat.
Engine Number	On nearside upper face of engine block forward of clutch housing.
Engine	4 Cylinder Single OHC
Bore of cylinder (mm)	79.96
Stroke (mm)	79.52
Cubic capacity	1597 cc/97.5 cu.in
Firing order	1-3-4-2
BHP (DIN @ RPM)	96 @ 6,000
Torque (Din ft/Lbs)	98 @ 4,000
Valve operation (or Clearances)	Hydraulic Tappets.

Valve Timing:

Inlet	8° BT	36° AB
Exhaust	34° BB	6° AT

Oil Capacity:

Engine (refill)	6.6 Imp Pts/8.0 US Pts/3.75 lts
Gearbox	2.6 Imp Pts/3.0 US Pts/1.5 lts
Rear axle	1.75 Imp Pts/2.1 US Pts/1.0 lts

Water capacity	13 Pts/7.4 lts
Cooling system	Water pump, radiator, thermostat and electric fan
Petrol	97 Octane
Tank capacity	*2-Seaters:* 8.5 Imp Gallons/10 US Gallons/39 lts *4-Seaters:* 10 Imp Gallons/12 US Gallons/45 lts

General Dimensions

Wheelbase	8' 244 cm
Track (front)	3' 11" 119 cm
Wire wheels	4' 122 cm
(rear)	4' 124 cm
Wire wheels	4' 1" 124 cm
Ground clearance	6¹/₂" 16 cm
Turning Circle	32' 10 metres
Tyre size	165/15 radials

Overall Dimensions

	2 Seater	4 Seater
Length	12' 366 cm	12' 366 cm
Width	4' 8" 142 cm	4' 8" 142 cm
Height (hood erected) ..	4' 3" 129 cm	4' 5" 135 cm

Body Dimension

Seat to Hood	3' 1" 94 cm	
	Front Seat	Rear Seat
	3' 2" 96 cm	2' 9" 84 cm
Width at Elbows	3' 10" 117 cm	
	Front Seat	Rear Seat
	3' 10" 117 cm	3' 9" 114 cm
Height of Seat from Floor	8" 20 cm	
	Front Seat	Rear Seat
	10" 25 cm	13" 33 cm
Leg Room	23" - 25" 58 cm - 63 cm	
		Rear Seat
		19" 48 cm
Door Width at Waistline	2' 3" 68 cm	

Luggage Space:

Length	3' 2" 96 cm
	Accommodation for hood,
Width	1' 4" min 40 cm
	tonneau and sidescreens
Depth	12" 30 cm

Weights

Complete with . . . . tools and petrol	1,580 lbs 718 kgs	1,660 lbs 750 kgs
Shipping weight	1,484 lbs 670 kgs	1,544 lbs 700 kgs

Ignition System

Initial Ignition Setting . .	12° BTDC
Spark Plug Types	Motorcraft AGP12C/AGPR12C
Spark Plug Gap	0.025/0.60
Contact Breaker Gap . .	Electronic Ignition

Carburetter

Type	Weber Twin Choke Down Draught 32/34 DFT

Front Wheel Alignment and Suspension

Castor angle	4°
Camber	2°
King Pin Inclination	2°
Toe-in	1/8" - 3/16" (3.2 mm to 4.8 mm)

Transmission

Clutch:	Diaphragm spring mechanical cable Operation Single Dry Plate
Clutch release arm free movement:	1/10" (2.54 mm)
Rear Axle:	Three-quarter floating, Hypoid crown wheel and pinion. Ratio 4.1:1
Gearbox:	Four Forward speeds all synchromesh. Floor remote change

Gear ratios

	Gearbox	Overall
1st	3.65	14.95
2nd	1.97	8.07
3rd	1.37	5.613
Top	1.00	4.10
Reverse	3.66	15.00

Performance Data (165/15 Tyres)

Miles per hour/1,000 rpm

4th	17.6
3rd	12.9
2nd	8.9
1st	4.8

DATA - FIAT ENGINE

Chassis Number	On offside top of cross member under front seat.
Engine Number	On nearside front to the engine block forward of above oil filter.
Engine	4 Cylinder Single OHC
Bore of cylinder (mm)	84
Stroke (mm)	71.5
Cubic capacity	1585 cc/96.68 cu.in
Firing order	1-3-4-2
BHP (DIN @ RPM)	8 @ 6,000
Torque (Din ft/Lbs)	94 @ 3,800
Valve operation	Inlet: 0.018 in 0.45 mm
(or Clearances)	Exhaust: 0.024 in 0.60 mm

Valve Timing: Inlet	12° BT	53° AB
Exhaust	54° BB	11° AT

Oil Capacity:

Engine (refill)	7.3 Imp Pts/8.8 US Pts/4.13 lts
Gearbox	3.2 Imp Pts/3.5 US Pts/1.8 lts
Rear axle	1.75 Imp Pts/2.1 US Pts/1.0 lts

Water capacity	13 Pts/7.4 lts
Cooling system	Water pump, radiator, thermostat and electric fan
Petrol	97 Octane
Tank capacity	*2-Seaters:*
	8.5 Imp Gallons/10 US Gallons/39 lts
	4-Seaters:
	10 Imp Gallons/12 US Gallons/45 lts

General Dimensions

Wheelbase	8' 244 cm
Track (front)	3' 11" 119 cm
Wire wheels	4' 122 cm
(rear)	4' 124 cm
Wire wheels	4' 1" 124 cm
Ground clearance	6¹/2" 16 cm
Turning Circle	32' 10 metres
Tyre size	165/15 radials

Overall Dimensions

	2 Seater	4 Seater
Length	12' 366 cm	12' 366 cm
Width	4' 8" 142 cm	4' 8" 142 cm
Height (hood erected) ..	4' 3" 129 cm	4' 5" 135 cm

Body Dimension

Seat to Hood	3' 1" 94 cm	
	Front Seat	Rear Seat
	3' 2" 96 cm	2' 9" 84 cm
Width at Elbows	3' 10" 117 cm	
	Front Seat	Rear Seat
	3' 10" 117 cm	3' 9" 114 cm
Height of Seat from Floor	8" 20 cm	
	Front Seat	Rear Seat
	10" 25 cm	13" 33 cm
Leg Room	23" - 25" 58 cm - 63 cm	
		Rear Seat
		19" 48 cm
Door Width at Waistline	2' 3" 68 cm	

Luggage Space:

Length	3' 2" 96 cm
	Accommodation for hood,
Width	1' 4" min 40 cm
	tonneau and sidescreens
Depth	12" 30 cm

Weights

Complete with . . . .　　1,580 lbs　718 kgs　　1,660 lbs　750 kgs
tools and petrol
Shipping weight . . . .　　　　1,484 lbs　670 kgs　1,544 lbs　700 kgs

Ignition System

Initial Ignition Setting . .　　10° BTDC
Spark Plug Types . . . . . .　　Champion N9Y/Marelli CW78LP
Spark Plug Gap . . . .　　0.024/0.60-0.70
Contact Breaker Gap . .　　Electric　　C.B. Type
　　　　　　　　　　　　　　0.30/0.40　　0.37/0.43

Carburetter

Type . . . .　　Weber Twin Choke
　　　　　　　　　　　　　　Down Draught 32 ADF

Front Wheel Alignment and Suspension

Castor angle . . . .　　4°
Camber . . . .　　2°
King Pin Inclination . . . . .　　2°
Toe-in . . . .　　1/8" - 3/16" (3.2 mm to 4.8 mm)

Transmission

Clutch:　　　　　　　　　　Diaphragm spring mechanical cable
　　　　　　　　　　　　　　Operation Single Dry Plate

Clutch release arm
　　free movement:　　　　1/10" (2.54 mm)
Rear Axle:　　　　　　　　Three-quarter floating, Hypoid
　　　　　　　　　　　　　　crown wheel and pinion. Ratio 4.1:1
Gearbox:　　　　　　　　　Five Forward speeds all
　　　　　　　　　　　　　　synchromesh.
　　　　　　　　　　　　　　Floor remote change
　　　　　　　　　　　　　　(do not lift for reverse)

Gear ratios

	Gearbox	Overall
1st	3.61	14.80
2nd	2.05	8.40
3rd	1.36	5.57
4th	1.00	4.10
5th	0.87	3.57
Reverse	3.24	13.28

Performance Data (165/15 Tyres)

Miles per hour/1,000 rpm

5th	20.2
4th	17.6
3rd	13.0
2nd	8.6
1st	4.9

Recommended Lubricants

These recommendations apply to temperate climates where operational temperatures may vary between approximately 10°F (-12°C) and 90°F (32°C). Information on recommended lubricants for use under extreme winter or tropical conditions can be obtained from the Morgan Motor Company or your local distributor.

Anti-freeze

It is essential that the level of anti-freeze should not fall below 40% at any time. Anti-freeze is required during winter and summer months to prevent corrosion of the aluminium engine components. The Anti-freeze used should be of a recommended type suitable for aluminium or mixed metal engines.

Recommended Lubricants

	CASTROL	MOBIL OIL	BP	SHELL	DUCKHAMS	TEXACO
Engine	Castrol GTX	Mobil Super	BP Visco Nova BP Visco 2000	Shell Super 15W/50	Hypergrade Oil	Havoline All Temperature 15W/40
Gearbox	Castrol SMX					
Rear Axle	Castrol Hypoy EP90	Mobilube HD90 or Mobilube SHC	BP Hypogear 90EP	Shell Spirax 90 EP	Hypoid 90S	Multigear EP 85W 90
Steering Box	Castrol Hypoy EP90	Mobilube HD90 or Mobilube SHC	BP Energrease FGL	Shell Spirax 90 EP	Hypoid 90S	Multigear EP 85W 90
Wheel Bearings	Castrol LM Grease	Mobilgrease MP or Mobilgrease Special	BP Energrease L2	Shell Retinax A	LB10	Multifak EP2 or Marfak All Purpose
Chassis grease points	Castrol MS3 Grease	Mobilgrease MP or Mobilgrease Special	BP Energrease L2	Shell Retinax A	LB10	Multifak EP2 or Marfak All Purpose
Oil Can	Castrol GTX	Engine Oil	Engine Oil	Shell Super 15W/50	Engine Oil	

INSTRUMENTS AND CONTROLS

Instruments

Speedometer

Indicates the vehicle speed and total mileage and is fitted with a trip which is cancelled by the knob (base of instrument face) when pressed.

Oil Pressure Gauge

This indicates the engine oil pressure. The oil pressure relief valve is set to return oil to the sump at a pressure of 35 - 40 lb^2 in for the Ford and 45 - 50 lb^2 in for the Fiat. When the engine is idling and at normal temperature the pressure will be lower than when running at a higher speed at the same temperature. Depending on the carburetter slow running adjustment, lubricant operating conditions and temperature, the idling pressure may drop to approx. 5 to 7 lb^2 in (0.35 to 0.4 kg^2 cm) at idling speed. If the gauge fails to register at normal running speeds then first check the engine oil level and if this is satisfactory, have the engine lubrication system examined immediately by your authorised dealer.

Voltmeter

This instrument indicates the condition of the battery on a voltmeter principle. A reading above the black sector which continues after 10 minutes running is too high and should be investigated. A reading below the black sector indicates the battery charging system requires attention.

Water Temperature Gauge

This is electrically operated, acting only when the ignition is switched on. The normal reading, is on or just above 90°C.

Fuel Gauge

Operates only when the ignition is on, the tank capacity is shown in the **General Specifications**.

Revolution Counter

Shows engine speed in revolutions per minutes and is calibrated in divisions of 100. It is of the electric impulse type.

Warning Light Unit (Placed centrally behind steering wheel):

(1) **Direction Indicator Monitor** The left-hand top indicator glows green when the steering column combination switch is moved to signal left-hand turn the right-hand indicator operates for a right-hand turn.

(2) **Hazard warning light (red)** Lights intermittently along with direction indicator warning light when hazard warning switch is operated.

(3) **Ignition Warning Light (red)** This serves the dual purpose of reminding the driver to switch off the ignition before leaving the vehicle and of acting as a no-charge indicator. With the ignition switch 'on', the warning light should be illuminated only when the engine is stopped or turning over very slowly. As the engine accelerates the light should dim and eventually go out at a fairly low engine speed. Failure of the light to behave in this fashion will indicate a broken alternator drive belt or other fault in the charging system.

(4) **Headlight Warning Light (blue)** Glows when headlights are on main beam, no light when dipped.

(5) **Brake Warning Light (red)** When the ignition is switched on with the handbrake applied the indicator should glow. Should failure of the front or rear brake lines occur or the brake fluid level be too low, the indicator will also light up.

FOOT OPERATED CONTROLS

Accelerator

The pedal is connected by a cable to the carburetter throttle. When starting from cold, depress the pedal fully. To engage the automatic choke, release the pressure and start.

Foot Brake Pedal

Actuates the brakes on all 4 wheels hydraulically, and also closes the circuit to the rear brake lights. These only operate when the ignition is switched on.

Clutch

Press pedal to disengage drive from engine to gearbox. DO NOT REST YOUR FOOT ON PEDAL WHEN DRIVING or hold the clutch out to freewheel as this will CAUSE UNNECESSARY WEAR.

HAND OPERATED CONTROLS

Handbrake

This is the 'fly-off' type. To operate the handbrake pull backwards, the lever is fixed in the 'on' position by pressing the cap on top of the lever which engages the pawl in the ratchet. To release brake pull the lever to the rear and allow to go forward to the full extent. Red warning light shows until handbrake is 'off'.

Heater valve control

Is operated by hand control situated to the left of the steering column. Push in for heating. Pull out to close water valve.

Combined light, direction indicator, horn, headlamp main beam and headlamp flasher control.

This antennae control is positioned on the right hand side of the steering column.

(a) **Direction Indicators** - Press the control downwards for right hand turns and lift upwards for left hand turns.

(b) **Headlamp Main Beam control** - With the headlamps on dipped-beam, push the control directly away from the steering wheel for main beam operation. The direction indicator can still be operated with the headlamp main beam in operation.

(c) **Headlamp Flasher Control** - Pull the control towards the steering wheel to flash the headlamps on to main beam. The control is spring-loaded and will return to its original position when released.

(d) **Horn Control** - To operate the horn, press the end of the control towards the steering column.

Windscreen wipers and washers

This control is effective only when the ignition is switched on.

For continuous operation of the two-speed wiper move the control downwards 'to position '1' for slow speed, or fully downwards to position '2' for high speed operation.

For single wipe action lift the control towards the steering wheel.

To operate the windscreen washers press the knob at the end of the control.

To switch off the wipers return the control to '0'. *Caution:* Always switch the wipers off before turning off the ignition. In frost or snow, always check that the wipers are free before operation. Not doing so will damage the wiper system. At all times use an additive in the washer system to prevent freezing. Do not use wipers on a dry screen.

Gear Lever

Always select neutral position before starting the engine.

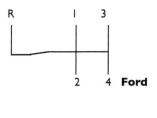

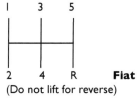

(Do not lift for reverse)

Steering Lock, Ignition and Starter Switch.

This switch is located on the steering column and has 4 positions.

Important: Take note of the key number.

1st position: Steering wheel lock in operation and ignition off, key can be extracted in this position.

2nd position Moving clockwise 'garage lock'. Ignition off, but steering unlocked which allows the car to be moved and steered by hand.

3rd position Ignition on.

4th position Is spring loaded and brings in the starter motor.

To prevent the starter being operated whilst the engine is running a safety device is incorporated whereby it is necessary to switch the key back to 'garage lock' position before the starter can be engaged. **Never allow the car to move unless the lock is released.**

Headlight, side and tail light switch.

This is a two position switch. First position side and tail lights together with number plate light and instrument light. Second position as above plus headlight.

Rear Red Fog Lamps.

These lights will only operate when other lights are switched on. The switch is only lit when the fog lamps are on.

DO NOT USE REAR FOG LAMPS IN GOOD WEATHER.

Hazard Switch.

This switch when depressed operates all direction lights and should only be used when the vehicle is stationery in an emergency situation.

Fan Heater Switch

Operates two speed fan blower motor in the car heater system.

Fog/Driving Light Switch

(Yellow) Operates both fog lights if required in adverse driving conditions (where fitted).

Instrument Illumination Rheostat.

Situated behind facia panel below voltmeter. Turn knob clockwise to illuminate the instruments at high intensity and anti-clockwise to reduce the intensity.

Seat Controls.

There are two types of seat available on the 4/4.

1:     Fixed Back Bucket
2:     Reclining

Both seats have forward and aft movement, controlled by the bar under the front of the seat cushion. The reclining seat has a fine adjusting knurled knob to give varying seat back angles, and also a lever to release the back so that it may be tilted to the fully forward position.

SEAT BELTS

Wearing

Never attempt to wear the belt other than as a complete lap and diagonal assembly. Do not try to use the belt for more than one person at a time, even with small children. Ensure that the belt webbing is not twisted when in use, and that the belt is adjusted to the correct tightness.

Using the harness

Remove the belt from the plastic parking device (integral with the top pillar anchorage on most cars, but supplied as a separate item with extra-long belts) draw the buckle over the shoulder

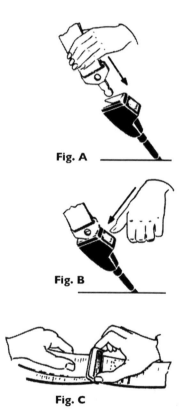

Fig. A

Fig. B

Fig. C

and across the chest and push it into the buckle unit nearest the wearer until a positive click ensures that the harness is safely locked (see fig A). To release the buckle press the red button on the buckle unit and stow away the belt (see fig B).

Adjusting

Adjustment is provided in the lap portion of the belt near the sill, or lower anchorage point. By tilting the adjuster upwards, the belt is then loosened, and may be lengthened or shortened accordingly, (see fig C). When the belt has been adjusted correctly there should be sufficient room to pass a hand between the chest and the webbing.

Cleaning the webbing

No chemical cleaners should be used on the webbing. If it becomes soiled, sponge with warm water, using a non-detergent soap, and allow to dry naturally, not by artificial heat or direct exposure to the sun.

NEVER ATTEMPT TO EITHER BLEACH OR RE-DYE THE WEBBING.

Warning:

1. Never at any time wear the lap belt loosely as this reduces its protection.

2. Periodically inspect the webbing for abrasion, paying particular attention to the anchorage points and adjusting devices.

3. In the event of an accident any safety belt which has been subject to a shock load should, in the interests of safety, be renewed

4. Alterations or additions to the kit which might impair the efficiency of the assembly should not be carried out. In the case of doubt, or suitability of a particular model, consult the manufacturers list.

RUNNING IN

During the first 30 hours or so of their working life, the moving parts of a new car require a 'bedding-in' or polishing process, such as is provided by light and medium running.

Long trouble-free life, particularly of engine, rear axle and brakes depends on this careful running-in, which can only be achieved by restraint on the part of those who drive the vehicle during its initial time.

The engine may seem to lack power for the first 200 to 300 miles (320-480 km) whilst this process is taking place. The power will then improve as the car is used for the first 2,000 miles (3,200 km), and this will be accompanied by a corresponding improvement in fuel consumption.

It is suggested that for the first 500 miles (800 km) engine speed should not be exceed 3,000 rpm.

Both long periods of idling and excessive racing of the engine should be avoided at all times and particularly during warming up from cold.

Do not allow the engine to 'labour' especially when driving up steep hills. At the first sign of this, change down, bearing in mind that changing down too early can result in undesirable racing of the engine.

Vary the rpm occasionally whenever possible, releasing the accelerator now and again to give the engine a better start in life.

As the machined surfaces approach their optimum condition, it becomes necessary to reset the adjustments to suit the more flexible engine. Your Morgan dealer will attend to this when he carries out the first 500 mile service.

SECTION TWO

Routine Maintenance and Adjustments

Notes on General Maintenance

In this section will be found information necessary to maintain your car in good mechanical condition in a temperate climate. Climatic and operating conditions affect maintenance intervals to a large extent; in many cases therefore, the determination of such intervals must be left to the good judgement of the owner or to advice from a Morgan distributor or dealer, but the recommendations will serve as a firm basis for maintenance work.

Important points

1. Depress the 'one shot' lubricator for a few seconds every 200 miles (550 km). Lubrication is preferable when the engine oil is cool.

2. Every 500 miles or weekly, whichever comes first, check the engine oil level, the radiator coolant level, windscreen and washer reservoir.

3. Every month check the tyre pressure and inspect tyre treads; when used for competitions or high speed touring check daily. Inspect front wheel tread wear and if uneven have wheel alignment checked. Check brake fluid level.

4. Owners are under a legal obligation to maintain all exterior lights in good working order; this also applies to headlamp beam setting, which should be checked at regular intervals by your garage.

Fuel recommendations

The engine is deigned to run on 97 Research octane fuel, 4-star grade in the United Kingdom.

LUBRICATION CHART

AT MILEAGE SHOWN

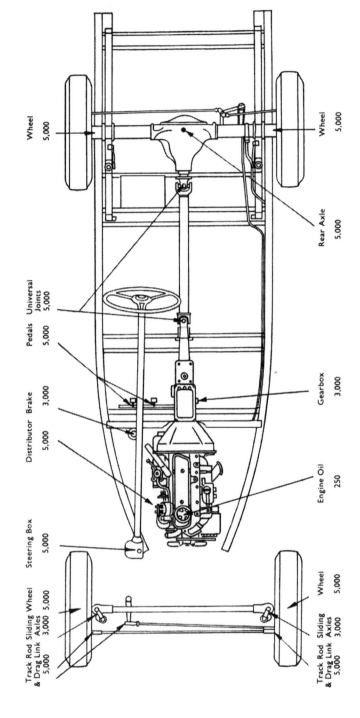

Track Rod Sliding Wheel
& Drag Link Axles 5,000
5,000 3,000

Steering Box 5,000

Distributor 5,000

Brake 3,000

Pedals 5,000

Universal Joints 5,000

Wheel 5,000

Wheel 5,000

Rear Axle 5,000

Gearbox 3,000

Engine Oil 250

Track Rod Sliding Wheel
& Drag Link Axles 5,000
5,000 3,000

Engine

Under adverse conditions such as driving over dusty roads or where short stop-start runs are made, oil changes, attention to the flame traps and breather filter replacement must be more frequent.

Air Cleaner and propeller shaft

When the car is driven over dusty or sandy roads the air cleaner should be changed more frequently and the propeller shaft serviced over shorter intervals to prevent ingress of abrasive materials.

Lubricants

Great importance is attached to the nature of lubricants used, and therefore specific recommendations are shown on page 16. Should for any reason these oils not be available in certain overseas territories, the Morgan distributor or dealer for the area will be able to recommend suitable alternatives.

Windscreen Washer

The water level in the windscreen washer should be checked every 500 miles (800 km). This is located on the bulkhead in the engine compartment on the opposite side to the steering column. Top up reservoir to within 1 in (25 mm) below top of orifice provided. Use a suitable all-weather windscreen washer additive, this will remove mud, flies and road film.

SECTION THREE

ENGINE

Engine Maintenance and Adjustments

Various adjustments are necessary from time to time in order to keep the mechanism in efficient running order. The period between depend largely upon the manner in which the car is used and no definite time can be given here for carrying out these corrections. The car should be examined, however, every 5,000 miles (8,000 km) and any adjustments which appear necessary can then be made.

Engine Lubrication

The engine oils recommended are of such a quality that the maintain sufficient body when hot, and are fluid enough to give early lubrication of the cylinder walls when starting up from cold.

Engine Oil Level

Engine oil level should be checked every 500 miles (800 km) or weekly whichever comes first. Stand the car on level ground and allow the oil to drain back into the sump. Withdraw the dipstick at right hand side of engine; wipe it clean and re-insert to its full depth and remove a second time to take the reading. Add oil as necessary through the oil filler at front of rocker cover.

Engine Oil Changes and Filter Replacements.

The engine oil and filter should be changed every 5,000 miles (8,000 km) or every six months. To change the oil; run the engine to normal temperature. Switch off the engine and remove drain plug from the bottom of the sump at the left hand side. Allow oil to drain away completely and replace the plug.

To Change Filter

Unscrew filter anti-clockwise and discard. Clean mounting face and screw new filter onto pump body until gasket just contacts pump. Tighten a further half a turn. Refill engine with approved oil to correct level. Clean and replace oil filler cap. Start engine and check for oil leaks. Stop engine, allow to stand and check oil level.

Weber Carburetter Slow Running Adjustment

The slow running adjustment should be carried out when the engine has reached its normal running temperature by screwing the hexagonal headed throttle screw in or out until the engine will run sufficiently fast not to stall and then adjust the round knurled headed petrol volume screw in and out until the engine runs evenly. If the engine is now running too fast, re-adjust the throttle screw anti-clockwise followed by a further slight adjustment on the petrol volume screw. Repeat these operations until idling engine revs are satisfactory.

This carburetter should require no further maintenance as it is of the fixed jet type. Do not expect a new engine to idle perfectly until the various machined surfaces have been 'run in'.

Fuel Pump

The fuel pump is located on the left hand side of the engine behind the oil filter or on the left in front of the carburetter. The pump is entirely automatic in action and requires little attention other than cleaning the nylon filter screen in the inverted metal dome on top of the pump every 5,000 miles. Occasionally the fuel line unions should be checked for tightness.

Sparking Plugs

The sparking plugs should be cleaned and gaps set (See pages 9 and 13), although for maximum efficiency it could be an advantage to renew the sparking plugs every 10,000 miles (16,000 km), ensure that the sparking plug insulators are clean to prevent 'HT' tracking.

Distribution Contact Points

Fiat

The contact breaker points gap should be adjusted (See page 13 for gap) by slackening off the locking screw on the fixed contact point and moving the contact point when the fibre arm of the moving contact is on the highest point of the cam. Securely tighten the lock screw and re-check the gap. If the points are worn or pitted, they should be dressed flat with an oil stone. By loosening the pinch clamp bolt at the base of the distributor and the adjusting bolt in the slot the ignition can be either advanced or retarded. Only small deviations from the normal setting are required and it is advisable to test the car on the road. Carefully note with a stop watch the time taken to accelerate from 20 mph (32 km) to 40 mph (64 km) (when 'run in' and subject to legal requirements) in top gear with the throttle fully open the optimum ignition setting is a that which gives the shortest time to accelerate.

Ford

Electronic ignition with no contact breaker.

Distributor maintenance

Fiat

Every 5,000 miles (8,000 km) the cam should be smeared lightly with engine oil. A pronounced squeak occurs when the cam is quite dry. Withdraw the moulded rotor arm from the top of the spindle (care should be taken because this part is made of brittle material), but do not remove the screw exposed to view. Apply by means of oil-can, a few drops of thin machine oil around the edge of the screw and down the hole provided, to lubricate the cam bearings and distributor spindle respectively. At the same time, place a single drop of clean engine oil on the contact breaker arm pivot. When replacing the rotor arm make sure that it is pushed on as far as possible. The moving parts of the automatic advance mechanism should be lubricated with winter grade engine oil. This can be squirted through the gap between the cam and the base plate. Take great care not to allow any oil to get on or near the contacts

Ford

No maintenance is required for the Ford type distributor, any problems should be referred to the Dealer.

Alternator Drive Belt Adjustment

Every 10,000 miles (16,000 km) check by thumb pressure between the alternator and crank shaft pulleys at midpoint. Movement should be $7/16$ to $9/16$ in (11 to 14 mm). If necessary adjust as follows:

1.   Slacken the bolts securing the alternator to the front cover; also the fixing at the adjustment link.

2.   Pivot the alternator inwards or outwards until the correct tension is obtained.

3.   Retighten the alternator adjusting bolts.

Clutch Adjustment

The amount of free movement on the clutch operating push rod should be $1/10$ in. Adjustment is made by slackening the lock nut at the base of the cable on the pedal end. Then turning the large adjusting nut clockwise or anti-clockwise as necessary. Do not forget to re-tighten the lock nut.

Front Suspension

Lubrication of the sliding axles is carried out by the 'one shot' lubrication system. The plunger which operates the system is situated in the top area on the left of the steering column above the driver's clutch foot on the scuttle. The plunger should be depressed every 200 miles (370 km), when the engine oil is cold. The plunger should be depressed for a few seconds during which time a very small decrease in the oil pressure may be noticed on the oil gauge.

The sliding axles are also provided with grease nipples which should be lubricated with grease every 5,000 miles (8,000 km). The grease helps to retain the oil supplied by the 'one shot' system.

The importance of frequent lubrication to the sliding axles cannot be too highly stressed as comfort is to a large extent dependent on the free working of these parts, and neglect will result in tightness which not only makes the springing harsh, but results in excessive wear, necessitating renewal before it should be necessary.

Steering

Check oil level in steering box every 5,000 miles (8,000 km), and top up with one of the recommended lubricants (page 16). Grease nipples are situated one at each end of the track rod and one at each end of the drag link and should be greased every 5,000 miles (8,000 km).

Should the steering become stiff a small amount of lubricating oil or grease on the steering friction dampers may prove beneficial.

Gearbox

The gearbox oil level should be checked every 3,000 miles (4,800 km) and topped up if necessary with the correct lubricant. A heavy oil or grease should not be used as this will spoil the operation of gear-changing.

An oil level and filler plug is situated on the left hand side of the gearbox and is accessible through a hole in the transmission cover forward from the front seat base. Top-up by means of an oil gun or suitable funnel and bring level of oil to the bottom of plug hole.

Rear Axle

It is essential to drain and replenish the axle with 'Hypoid' oil every 5,000 miles (8,000 km). A drain plug is provided at the base of the axle.

The hypoid bevel gears fitted in the rear axle require a special lubricant to ensure efficient operation and long life.

The type of gear incorporates a sliding action between the exceptionally sturdy gear teeth, resulting in silent operation. However, the rubbing action is too severe for normal oils, special 'Hypoid' oils have been developed which contain additives that make the oil capable of withstanding pressures many times heavier than normal oils can cope with. A further feature of 'Hypoid' oils is that they are 'lighter' - that is to say, more fluid than normal axle oils. However, the special additives begin to lose their properties in the course of use, and the oil tends to revert to a light gear oil.

Thus it is advisable to completely drain and replenish with a new 'Hypoid' oil every 5,000 miles (8,000 km), and in any event do not exceed a period of 10,000 miles (16,000 km).

It is desirable to have the oil level checked during this period and if the oil level is below the plug on the rear do not 'top up' but drain the oil and refill with new oil, this will overcome the danger of mixing the various grades of oil.

Clean away grit from filler plug and refill until oil reaches the level of the filler plug on the rear of the axle case.

Rear Road Spring

The rear road springs should be painted or sprayed with engine oil very 5,000 miles (8,000 km).

It is the area around the tips of the blades which most requires the lubricant, as it is at these points that one blade presses upon the next. The spring clip should also be oiled.

Oil should be kept away from the rubber bushes located at each end of each spring.

Other Lubricating Points

The following items should be oiled at least at each major service, to prevent unnecessary wear:

Rear brake yoke pins, and balance lever pivots.
Door hinges and locks.
Bonnet catches and tape seating.
Accelerator linkage.
Wheel studs (to prevent rusting).
Steering damper blades.

Brake fluid reservoir.

The brake fluid reservoir is situated under the bonnet on the bulkhead on the same side of the car as the driver.

Every 5,000 (8,000 km) remove the cover and check fluid level in the reservoir. If necessary replenish to within $1/2$ in. (12 mm) of the top with Castrol Girling Crimson Brake and Clutch Fluid (SAE70OR3). Replace cover ensuring that the rubber sealing ring is in good condition and that the ventilation hole is unblocked.

If significant topping-up is required check master cylinder, slave cylinders and pipes for leakage; any leakage must be rectified immediately.

After approximately 3 years or 40,000 miles (64,000 km) the seals and cups of the hydraulic system should be inspected and if necessary replaced.

Brakes

The brakes will be inspected regularly during normal servicing, but should the car be used for competition work, brake wear will be much more rapid and therefore inspection and perhaps replacement of pads or shoes may be necessary during the period in between.

Cleanliness is essential when dealing with brakes, as no method is known of successfully removing grease or oil from brake linings. Always replace with genuine Morgan relined shoes or pads as they will have the correct grade of lining, ground to the correct contour and inspected to conform to the original specification.

Front Brake Pads

Hydraulic disc brakes are fitted to the front wheels and the correct brake adjustment is automatically maintained, no provision is therefore made for adjustment.

Every 5,000 miles (8,000km) (more frequently if used in competition), check the thickness of the brake pads and renew if the minimum thickness is less than 1/8" (3 mm). Also check for oil contamination of brake pads and discs.

Front Brake Pads - Removal

1. Jack up front of the car and remove wheels.

2. Remove hairpin clips and withdraw the pad retaining pins.

3. Withdraw the pads complete with anti-rattle springs and damping shims.

4. Measure the lining material and if less than 3 mm renew the pads. If pads are not to be replaced, mark them in order so they can be replaced in the original position.

Replacement

1. Push in the pistons with an even pressure to the bottom of the cylinder bores. Then slide the pads into position, together with the damping shims. Ensure arrow cut-out in shim points in direction of rotation.

2. Refit the anti-rattle springs if included, one on each pad then replace the pad retaining pins, ensuring that the anti-rattle springs are clipped under the pins. Fit new hairpin clips.

3. Pump the foot brake pedal until a solid resistance is felt. This repositions the pistons and puts the pads in slight friction contact with the disc.

4. Refit the road wheels, remove the car from the jack & road test car.

Rear Brake Drums

The Hydraulic brake drums are fitted to the rear wheels and should be inspected and checked every 5,000 miles (8,000 km) or before if the brake pedal has excessive free movement. To adjust proceed as follows:

1. Jack up rear of vehicle and remove rear wheels, (the last operation is not essential but makes the task easier).

2. Turn the adjuster nut in a clockwise direction until the shoes contact the drum and release back one or two notches until the drum is free. The single adjuster is placed facing in a forward direction on the backplate.

Rear Brake Shoe Replacement

1.   Jack up car and remove rear road wheels.

2.   Remove countersunk screw and take off brake drum.

3.   Dismantle the brake by prising one shoe out of the groove in the wheel cylinder piston with a large screwdriver. Both shoes and pull off springs can now be removed, leaving the wheel cylinders and pivot pins in position on the backplate. Do not detach these units from the backplate. To prevent loss of brake fluid, place an elastic band over the wheel cylinder pistons to hold these in place.

4.   Clean down back plate and check the wheel cylinder for leaks and freedom of motion. It is important that the adjuster is turned back (anti-clockwise) to the full 'off' position and is working freely.

5.   To fit replacement shoes, first attach shoe springs (new if possible) to shoes. Be sure that the springs are between the shoe webs and backplate, otherwise shoes will not be flat on the backplate. Keep all grease off linings and do not handle linings more than necessary. Place shoes with springs attached against backplate. Shoes have half round slots at one end. Fit these slots to the pivot pin, then insert the other end of the shoe in the wheel cylinder piston. Place the screwdriver under the web of the remaining shoe and against the backplate. Ease the shoes into the grooves on the piston.

6.   Refit drums; be sure these are clean and free from grease, etc.

7.   Tighten up adjusters until the wheel just locks and then slacken off until the wheel spins freely.

8.   Refit road wheels, jack down and road test.

The Handbrake

Adjustment of the rear brake shoes automatically re-adjusts the handbrake mechanism. The rods are correctly set before leaving the works and only maladjustment will result from tampering with the mechanism. Cable adjustment may be made by turning the adjuster at the rear of the handbrake cable.

The lever compensating mechanism on the rear axle should be kept free and well oiled.

Bleeding the System

Except for periodical inspection of the fluid level in the reservoir chamber and lubrication of the handbrake cables and connections, no attention should be necessary. If, however, a pipe joint is uncoupled at any time, or the wheel cylinder cups are inspected or replaced, the system must be bled in order to expel any air which may have been admitted.

Air is compressible, and its presence in the system will affect the working of the brakes.

1. Wipe clean the bleeder nipple of the brake concerned and fit a piece of rubber tube over it, allowing the tube to hang in a clean container partially filled with fluid, so that the end of the pipe is below the level of the fluid.

2. Unscrew the bleeder nipple one complete turn with a suitable spanner. There is only one bleeder nipple to each wheel.

3. The fluid reservoir of the master cylinder must be topped up before commencing the bleeding operation, and must be kept at least half filled during the whole operation, otherwise more air will be drawn into the system via the master cylinder. Always clean the area around the screwed cap before removing it, this will lessen the risk of grit falling into the chamber after removal.

4.	Depress the brake pedal quickly and allow it to return without assistance. Repeat this pumping operation with a slight pause between each depression of the pedal. Observe the flow of fluid being discharged into the glass jar and when all air bubbles cease to appear, hold the pedal firmly down and securely tighten the bleeder nipple.

Note:

Depending upon the position at which a pipe joint has been uncoupled it will be necessary to bleed the system at either both front or both rear wheels. If the pipe was uncoupled at the master cylinder then the system must be bled at all four wheels.

Battery

The battery fitted is a 12 volt 36 amp/hr battery with negative earthing. Keep the terminals clean and well covered with petroleum jelly. If they are corroded, scrape them clean, assemble and cover with petroleum jelly. Wipe away all dirt and moisture from the top of the battery, and make sure that the connections are clean.

Wheels and Tyres

In the normal course of wear and tear, or due to minor impacts, the wheels may develop irregularities, or cease to point directly in the direction of motion. A check should be made periodically to ensure that the wheels are in correct alignment or 'track'. Every garage possesses an alignment gauge and can carry out a test in a few moments. Errors in alignment can be corrected by adjustment of the track rod, the ends of which are threaded for this purpose. The 'Toe-in' for the front wheels should be $^1/8$"- $^3/16$". 'Toe-in', even in the smallest degree, is to be avoided.

To ensure smooth running especially on the front wheels and at high speeds, it is recommended that wheels and tyres are periodically balanced, this can be carried out by most garages, and the trouble in having this done is well repaid by the results obtained.

Pressures:

Tyre pressures should be checked weekly and at every maintenance inspection. Maximum life and performance will only be obtained if the tyres are maintained at correct pressures.

	lbs/sq in.	kg/cm^2
Normal (front and rear)	18	1.26
High speed (front and rear)	24	1.68

Wherever possible check with the tyres cold, as the pressure is about 3 lbs/sq in. (0.2 kg/cm^2) higher at running temperature. Always replace the valve caps, as they form a positive seal on the valves.

When high speed touring or taking part in competitions, the tyre pressures should be checked much more frequently, even to the extent of a daily check.

Any unusual pressure loss (in excess of 1 lb/sq in (0.5 kg/cm^2) per week) should be investigated and corrected.

Always check spare the wheel, so that it is ready for use at any time.

At the same time remove embedded flints, etc., from the tyre treads with the aid of a penknife or similar tool.

Wheel and tyre units are accurately balanced if necessary on initial assembly with the aid of clip-on weights secured to the wheel rims.

Tyres must be replaced with those of the same specification and quality originally fitted. Do not drive on tyres or wheels showing any sign of wear or damage. Tyres must be replaced as soon as the wear indicator in the tread is level with any part of the tread. Worn tyres are dangerous, especially on a performance car. They may cause changes in the handling, particularly in wet conditions. Always maintain the correct pressures and wheel alignment. Always check pressure when the tyres are cold.

Wheel Balance

When tyres are changed, road wheels should be carefully checked for possible damage.

When replacements are required, the tyres should be as currently specified by the Company. They should be of the same type as those previously fitted.

Headlamp beam setting

This operation should be carried out every 10,000 miles (16,000 km), but is best left in the hands of your garage. They can however be set reasonably accurately as follows:

Place the car 25 ft (7.6 m) away from a blank wall, taking care that the car stands on a level surface, and that the front of the car is parallel to the wall. The car must be unladen. Do this job at night, or pick a spot which is well shaded, so that the light spots thrown by the lamps can be clearly seen. When correctly set the light spots from the lamps should be 2½" (63 mm) below the centre of the headlamps. The beams should also be parallel with each other. If they require adjustment, remove the moulding surrounding the lamp – and the beam adjustment screws will be exposed.

The top screw controls vertical adjustment and the lower screw the horizontal adjustment. It is preferable to start with the screws well in so that the moulding does not interfere with them when replaced.

Headlights

The headlights are of the Halogen type with H4 12 volt clear bulbs (export yellow).

To renew the headlight bulb, remove the moulding surrounding the lamp. Place two fingers in the holes at the bottom of the rim and pull towards the front of the car.

Remove the lamp, grip the lense and reflector firmly on each side and pull with a steady pressure. Remove rubber cover and clip, then bulb.

Fuse Box

The fuse box is located on top of the scuttle. The cover is a snap fit and when removed will reveal 4 fuses and two spares.

Fuses

Fuse (35 amp) in holder marked 1 and 2 is for side lights, rear lights and driving lights.

Fuse (35 amp) in holder marked 3 and 4 is for constant current auxiliaries, i.e: horn, head light flasher. The spare fuses are both 35 amp.

Fuse (2 amp) in holder marked 5 and 6 and Fuse (15 amp) in holder marked 7 and 8 are for ignition and axillaries, i.e: screen wipers, washer, heater, stop lights.

Facia Lights

Illuminated facia panel bulbs. Ensure the correct light bulbs are fitted as follows:

Warning light unit behind steering wheel 12v 1.5W
Light bulbs in switches 14v 0.56W

Caution: Always be certain to use the correct specification of bulb, particularly in dashboard switches and instruments.

High Tension Cables

High tension cables should be renewed if signs of cracking or perishing appear. These can be obtained as a set from your Morgan/Lucas Agent or an individual lead can be replaced. Only 7 mm PVC or Neoprene covered rubber insulated ignition cable should be used.

Front Suspension Damper Blades

On certain cars which have covered considerable mileage, faults are sometimes noticed in respect of front wheel vibration even though the wheels are correctly balanced. This can be overcome by making sure that the flat spring sheet blade mounted from the stub axle to the chassis side member is secured without any radial movement at the chassis end. This blade should slide inwards and outwards only. Any sideways or radial movement should be reduced to a minimum by adjusting the shims. These shims are locked in place by the two bolts which secure the flat steel clamps to the chassis. It may also be necessary to renew the damper blades if worn edges are apparent. These blades should be greased regularly.

Coachwork

It is recommended that the paintwork should not be treated with a heavy wax for a period of three months after the car has been painted. This will allow the paintwork to 'breathe' and cure correctly.

This is assuming **normal** driving conditions i.e. the car being used and not stored under cover. If the car is rarely used we would increase this time to anything up to six months.

For removing any imperfections, such as scratches should be removed, using good quality fine grade rubbing compound applied with a soft cloth. This should be used until the scratch has disappeared (being careful not to polish all the colour away - unlikely knowing how much paint is on the car to start with!)

This should then be followed with top quality polish or high-end fine polishing cream.

A good quality a fine cutting abrasive polish for general polishing and for restoring aged paint films and removing traffic film can be used.

After the time intervals we have stated it would be alright to wax polish a car - use a recognised cream wax and generally try to keep away from silicon polishes and sealants as they tend to seal the paint and prevent it 'breathing' - problems can also arise when refinishing the paint surface.

Hood

When erecting the hood, always fix the eyelets in the back curtain over the turn-buttons first and then fix snaps across the top of the windscreen, starting in the centre, making sure the sealing pipe runs along the back of the screen. If secured at the front first some strain will be necessary to pull the eyelets over the turn-buttons, which in time will pull away from the fabric.

However, it is recommended that if the hood is tight when dismantling it is advisable to release it at the turn-buttons, which avoids straining at the eyelets. It is not intended that the tonneau cover over the rear compartment should remain in position when the hood is up as the turn-buttons do not allow for the double thickness, and unnecessary strain is placed on the hood fabric and turn-buttons alike.

Before cleaning, it is advisable to run a little light oil along the piping between the wings and the body. This will help to keep the wax sealant used fluid and prevent water entering the seams. The excess can be washed off and the car cleaned in the normal way.

Side Curtains

It should be remembered that Vybak is easily scratched and soiled, spoiling vision at the sides. When not in use, therefore, do not throw the sidescreens carelessly into the rear compartment or they may move about and become damaged. A small 'tommy bar' is provided to facilitate the tightening of the knurled knob fixing the sidescreens to the car.

Hydraulic Dampers

The telescopic piston type dampers fitted to front and lever type rear respectively should not require any attention such as 'topping-up'. They should however be kept as clean and free from oil and dirt as possible so that heat generated by their normal function will dissipate quickly.

Jacking System

The jack is used in the following manner:

First make sure that the car cannot move backwards or forwards by using the brakes or chocking the car firmly.

The jack may be used for lifting front wheels by placing it under the bottom cross axle tube, care should be taken not to damage the brake pipe.

Rear wheels can be lifted by using the jack directly under the rear chassis box cross member.

Great care must be taken if the car has to be lifted on cambered surfaces. No work other than changing wheels must take place under the vehicle unless the car is standing on proper supports that are fully capable of withstanding the full weight. No part of a person's anatomy must be under the car when the jack is used for any purposes.

Wiring Diagram

COLOUR CODING

B	BLACK
BG	BLACK/GREEN
BO	BLACK/ORANGE
BW	BLACK/WHITE
G	GREEN
GB	GREEN/BLACK
GLG	GREEN/LIGHT GREEN
GN	GREEN/BROWN
GP	GREEN/PURPLE
GR	GREEN/RED
GU	GREEN/BLUE
GW	GREEN/WHITE
LG	LIGHT GREEN
N	BROWN
NLG	BROWN/LIGHT GREEN
NB	BROWN/BLACK
NG	BROWN GREEN
NP	BROWN/PURPLE
NW	BROWN/WHITE
NU	BROWN/BLUE
NY	BROWN/YELLOW
PB	PURPLE/BLACK
U	BLUE
ULG	BLUE/LIGHT GREEN
UR	BLUE/RED
UW	BLUE/WHITE
UY	BLUE/YELLOW
R	RED
RB	RED/BLACK
RU	RED/BLUE
RW	RED/WHITE
RY	RED/YELLOW
W	WHITE
WLG	WHITE/LIGHT GREEN
WB	WHITE/BLACK
WR	WHITE/RED
WY	WHITE/YELLOW
Y	YELLOW
YS	YELLOW/GREEN

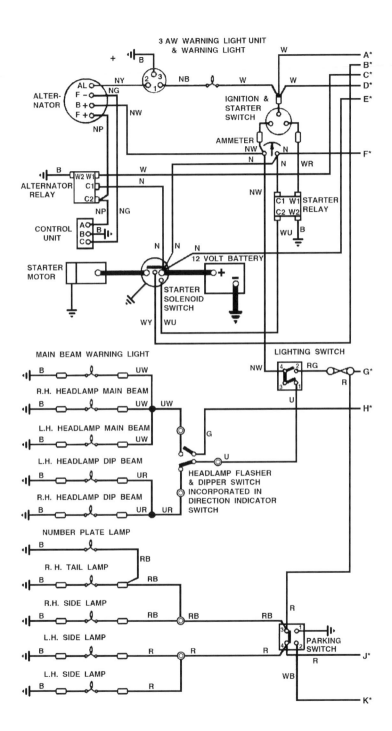

3 AW WARNING LIGHT UNIT & WARNING LIGHT

ALTERNATOR

IGNITION & STARTER SWITCH

AMMETER

ALTERNATOR RELAY

CONTROL UNIT

STARTER MOTOR

STARTER RELAY

STARTER SOLENOID SWITCH

12 VOLT BATTERY

MAIN BEAM WARNING LIGHT

R.H. HEADLAMP MAIN BEAM

L.H. HEADLAMP MAIN BEAM

L.H. HEADLAMP DIP BEAM

R.H. HEADLAMP DIP BEAM

HEADLAMP FLASHER & DIPPER SWITCH INCORPORATED IN DIRECTION INDICATOR SWITCH

LIGHTING SWITCH

NUMBER PLATE LAMP

R. H. TAIL LAMP

R.H. SIDE LAMP

L.H. SIDE LAMP

L.H. SIDE LAMP

PARKING SWITCH

A* B* C* D* E* F* G* H* J* K*

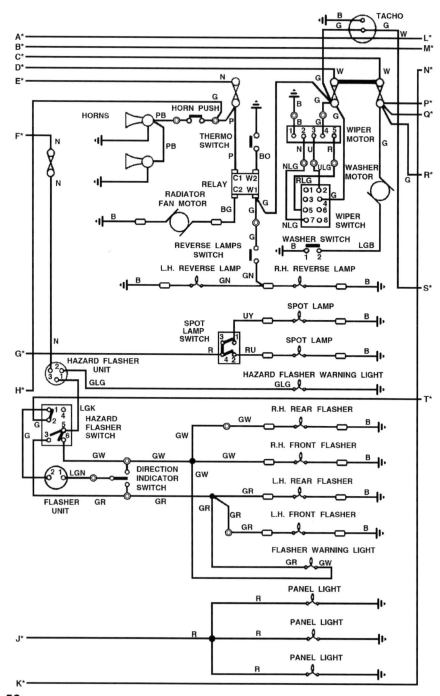

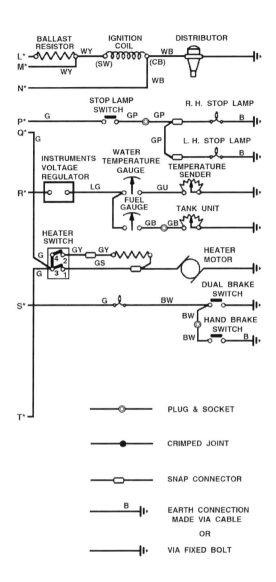

BALLAST RESISTOR
IGNITION COIL
DISTRIBUTOR

L*
M*
WY
(SW)
WB
(CB)
WB
N*

STOP LAMP SWITCH
R. H. STOP LAMP

P*   G   GP   GP   B
Q*   G
                GP   L. H. STOP LAMP
                        B

INSTRUMENTS VOLTAGE REGULATOR
WATER TEMPERATURE GAUGE
TEMPERATURE SENDER

R*   LG   GU
FUEL GAUGE   TANK UNIT
               GB   GB

HEATER SWITCH
G   GY   GY
4 2   GS
3 1
G

HEATER MOTOR

DUAL BRAKE SWITCH

S*   G   BW
               BW   HAND BRAKE SWITCH
               BW   B

T*

⊙   PLUG & SOCKET

●   CRIMPED JOINT

▭   SNAP CONNECTOR

B ⏚   EARTH CONNECTION MADE VIA CABLE

OR

⏚   VIA FIXED BOLT

SERVICE

Our Service Department is especially equipped to take care of customers requirements, and can at all times undertake anything from adjustments to major repairs and complete overhauls, at reasonable charges consistent with expert workmanship.

Parts sent for repairs must be consigned carriage paid and should be clearly labelled with the sender's name and address, along with chassis and engine number.

Instructions should be sent separately whether an estimate is required before putting the work in hand. When it is inconvenient to send repairs to the works an accredited 'Morgan' Dealer should be consulted.

SERVICE HISTORY

FIRST SERVICE

After 1,000 miles (1,500 km) or 3 months after delivery

Serviced by: Name: ....

                  Address: ....

                               ....

                               ....

Date:.............   Mileage ....

Signature   ....

SECOND SERVICE

At 5,000 miles (8,000 km) or 6 months after delivery

Serviced by: Name: ....

                  Address: ....

                               ....

                               ....

Date:.............   Mileage ....

Signature   ....

THIRD SERVICE

At 10,000 miles (16,000 km) or 12 months after delivery

Serviced by: Name: ....

                   Address: ....

                            ....

                            ....

Date:.............   Mileage ....

Signature   ....

FOURTH SERVICE

At 15,000 miles (24,000 km) or 12 months after delivery

Serviced by: Name: ....

                   Address: ....

                            ....

                            ....

Date:.............   Mileage ....

Signature   ....

FIFTH SERVICE

At 20,000 miles (32,000 km) or 24 months after delivery

Serviced by: Name: ....

Address: ....

....

....

Date: ....   Mileage ....

Signature   ....

SIXTH SERVICE

At 25,000 miles (40,000 km) or 30 months after delivery

Serviced by: Name: ....

Address: ....

....

....

Date: ....   Mileage ....

Signature   ....

SEVENTH SERVICE

At 30,000 miles (48,000 km) or 36 months after delivery

Serviced by: Name: ....

                      Address: ....

                               ....

                               ....

Date:.............   Mileage ....

Signature   ....

EIGHTH SERVICE

At 35,000 miles (56,000 km) or 42 months after delivery

Serviced by: Name: ....

                      Address: ....

                               ....

                               ....

Date:.............   Mileage ....

Signature   ....

NINTH SERVICE

At 40,000 miles (64,000 km) or 48 months after delivery

Serviced by: Name: ....

                 Address: ....

                           ....

                           ....

Date: ....   Mileage ....

Signature   ....

TENTH SERVICE

At 45,000 miles (72,000 km) or 54 months after delivery

Serviced by: Name: ....

                 Address: ....

                           ....

                           ....

Date: ....   Mileage ....

Signature   ....

NOTES

NOTES

NOTES

NOTES

WARRANTY

The Morgan Motor Company Limited warrants in respect of its parts supplied and which is returned to the Company's premises at Pickersleigh Road, Malvern Link, Worcestershire, within 12 months that it will examine the same and should any fault due to defective materials or manufacture be found upon such examination, to repair or replace the defective part without charge, at the Company's discretion.

Any part manufactured other than by the Company is protected by the warranty (if any) given by that manufacturer and the Company can accept no responsibility save and except in accordance with any such warranty. It is a condition of this warranty that the vehicle must not have been neglected, misused, modified or used for racing or rallying and that it has been serviced in accordance with the recommendations of the Company as embodied within this handbook or otherwise defined.

The warranty does not apply to tyres or consumables (e.g. brake pads/shoes, clutch lining, etc.) or to defects arising from the fitting of parts not made by or approved by the Company or by the original manufacturers of any proprietary parts fitted to the vehicle.

Any parts or parts replaced or repaired under this warranty will be covered for the balance of the warranty period.

The warranty is dependent upon compliance by the vehicle owner with the following provisions:

a) The owner shall send to the Company's premises such part or parts as are alleged to be defective promptly on discovery of the claimed defect. Transportation is to be prepaid and the part or parts to be properly packed and clearly marked for identification with the full name and address of the owner and with the car and chassis numbers of the vehicle from which the parts have been taken.

b) The owner shall post to the Company on or before despatch of such parts as are alleged to be defective a full and complete description of the claim and the reasons therefore.

c) In the event of any disagreement the matter shall be referred to the decision of an agreed arbitrator or in the event of failure to agree an arbitrator to be appointed by the President for the time being of The Law Society.

This assurance is in addition to and does not detract from the contractual rights you have under Statute or at common law.

Index

Morgan Motor Company Limited
Pickersleigh Road, Malvern Link, Worcestershire.
WR14 2LL England
Tel: 01684 573104 / 573105   www.morgan-motor.co.uk

Whilst every effort is made to ensure the accuracy of the particulars contained in this book neither the manufacturing companies, publishers nor the distributors will not, in any circumstances, be held liable for any inaccuracies or the consequences thereof.

Brooklands Books Ltd., PO Box 146, Cobham,
Surrey KT11 1LG, England Phone: (44) 1932 865051
E-mail: sales@brooklands-books.com   www.brooklands-books.com

ISBN 9781783181858   Ref: MORFF   9T6/2732

Printed in Great Britain
by Amazon